The Spirits of Athens

The Spirits of Athens

HAUNTING TALES OF AN ALABAMA TOWN

SHANE BLACK

iUniverse, Inc.
New York   Bloomington

The Spirits of Athens
Haunting Tales of an Alabama Town

iUniverse books may be ordered through booksellers or by contacting:

iUniverse
1663 Liberty Drive
Bloomington, IN 47403
www.iuniverse.com
1-800-Authors (1-800-288-4677)

ISBN: 978-1-4401-7776-7 (sc)
ISBN: 978-1-4401-7775-0 (ebk)

Printed in the United States of America

iUniverse rev. date: 10/01/2009

All of the author's profits from the sale of this book will be donated to the Spirit of Athens, Inc. The Spirit of Athens is a non-profit organization dedicated to the renovation, revitalization, and future growth of the downtown area in the city of Athens, Alabama. More information about the Spirit of Athens can be found at www.spiritofathens.com.

Table of Contents

Preface

I need to make a confession before I write another word: I don't believe in ghosts.

Well, that's not exactly true – I certainly believe in the Holy Ghost. But, as a rule, I don't believe in unearthly phantoms of the departed lingering on our mortal plane, manifesting themselves, and scaring the wits out of us. I think there are more pressing things going on in the afterlife.

Having issued that disclaimer, it may then seem strange that I accepted a challenge to write this book about ghost stories in my hometown of Athens, Alabama. The reason I accepted is that while I don't believe in ghosts, I do emphatically believe in three things that make this book seem very worthwhile.

First of all, I love the telling of a good story. I'm not alone in that sentiment here in Athens. As good Southerners, we all love to listen to the old-timers on front porches weave spellbinding tales that will sometimes make the hairs on the backs of our necks stand straight up.

Second, I believe in preserving local folklore. Too many times good stories are lost and fade away into the pages of history with no record left behind. That's the only way a story dies, you know – when the voices that tell it are hushed forever – and it's a tragic thing when that happens.

Finally, although I am a skeptic when it comes to ghosts, I must admit that something strange is going on here. I believe that a significant number of sincere, rational folks in this town have indeed had weird things happen to them that are just plain inexplicable. I know many of these good people personally, and I find it impossible to disclaim their experiences out of hand.

When I worked with Jeanette Dunnavant at the Greater Limestone County Chamber of Commerce to begin compiling ghost stories in and around Athens, I was amazed by the sheer number of them. Although most of them involved general occurrences (like footsteps in a hall, frightened cats, or bumps in the night), there were many that were surprisingly specific in detail. I was also amazed at the number of these stories that seemed to focus on places in and around downtown. While I regret the omission of other tales in the area (like the ghostly organ that can be heard in north Athens at the site of a burned church building), I've attempted in these pages to bring you the best of the stories from the heart of town.

So, I hope that you enjoy the tall tales within this book, and that they sufficiently arm you with information to share around a campfire at Lucy's Branch, on a front porch in Ripley, or maybe on the lawn of McCandless Hall on a dark Halloween night. And as you read through these chapters, take care to repeat to yourself what I did to myself as I interviewed the witnesses who recounted these tales.

"I don't believe in ghosts. I don't believe in ghosts. I don't believe in ghosts."

Full moon above the old Athens Cemetery.
Photo by Alissa Rose-Clark.

Acknowledgments

This book wouldn't be possible without the help and support of lots of people, and I'd like to take a moment to thank them. Thanks to my family (Trisha, Gayle, and the kids) for their support and advice. Thanks to Alissa Rose-Clark for her spectacular photographs. Thank you to Randi Harbin and Charlotte Fulton for their advice and editorial comment. Thanks to Jeanette Dunnavant, Gina Yarbrough, and Michelle Williamson for their research and technical support. Thanks to Garth Lovvorn, Sr., Garth Lovvorn, Jr., Ruby Lovelace, Pat Lewis, Don Ussery, Amy Steele, Kristin Black, and Sara Love for sharing some wonderful source material.

Also, thank you to Faye Axford, Chris Edwards, Robert Dunnavant, Jr., Frank G. Westmoreland, Jr., Robert Henry Walker, Jr., Elva Bell McLin, Joe H. Slate, Jacquelyn Reeves, Sandra Stockton, James Crowley Smith, Mary Fielding, George C. Bradley, and Richard L. Dahlen, whose personal, folklore, historical and scholarly writings provided valuable references for the material in this book. I recommend their works to the reader.

Special thanks is also owed to *The Athens News Courier*, the Limestone County Archives, and the Limestone County Historical Society, whose dutiful preservation of the city of Athens' rich history makes all works like this possible. Similarly, thank you to the Donnell House Board, Inc., the George S. Houston Library and House Board, and Athens State University for their preservation of many of the significant and historical buildings referenced in this book.

No child in Alabama raised during the 1970s could resist Kathryn Tucker Windham's "13 Alabama Ghosts and Jeffrey." That book certainly inspired this one. Thank you, Mrs. Windham.

Finally, thanks to the many folks who, after hearing some of the spooky tales in this book, said, "Hey, you need to write those down on paper before they are forgotten." This book is dedicated to those people.

Introduction

The city of Athens, Alabama, is a picturesque, quintessential Southern town in north central Alabama. It is an old town, as far as Alabama towns go, having been founded in 1818. Its people are hardy. Over their history, they've weathered tornadoes, infernos, typhoid epidemics, a military invasion, and even a nuclear near-disaster. They're also proud. In the early 1900s, the people rejected a Confederate soldier memorial because his head was turned downwards, perhaps signaling defeat, and so they spared no expense in moving it to the graveyard and erecting a new and different statue altogether. They're a devout people. There are churches on almost every corner, many with families in their congregations who have sat in the same pew for generations.

The city has been a cotton town, a temperance town, a railroad town, a wet town, and it is now a growing town. The town's population is estimated at 23,000 plus, and it is expected to expand rapidly in the near future due to nearby commercial development. It is a city poised on the edge between tradition and progress.

In recent years, there has been a tremendous civic focus on revitalizing downtown Athens. New retailers and restaurants are bursting open like spring dogwoods on the town square. Local civic leaders and promoters are spending considerable time organizing events, such as storytelling conventions and music festivals. In 2006, I was contacted to assist the local chamber of commerce in developing an Athens "ghost tour" to offer a family-friendly event during late October.

Although a lawyer (not a ghost-hunter) by trade, and a skeptic (not a ghost-believer) by nature, I agreed to assist in researching and assembling the information needed for such an event. During this work, I was amazed – not by generic anecdotes about hissing cats, cold spots, and self-opening doors – but by the rich history and background behind some of the strange tales we discovered. Apparently, I was not the only one enamored with the local folklore, as our first few ragtag tours sold out within a few days of being offered to the public.

Most of the ghost stories are rooted in the town's local history. For the most part, one just can't tell these stories without also revealing something special about Athens. For example, one cannot relate the tale of the ghost child of the Donnell House without also explaining how that girl had been literally *frightened to death* by marauding Union soldiers during the Civil War invasion of Athens. Similarly, the tale of the phantom grandfather clock in the George S. Houston Library and House cannot be shared without discussing Athens' own Governor Houston and how he rescued the state from bankruptcy. Likewise, the narrative about the two ghosts struggling to escape an inferno on the town square cannot be recited without telling about the catastrophe that finally led city fathers to install a public water system.

These stories are also heterogeneous in their ghostly elements – that is to say, they form an interesting mix of "supernatural stuff." There is, for example, the recurring, thunderous BOOM on the floor of McCandless Hall's auditorium representing the fatal fall of a young lover. Another tale speaks of the ghostly images of Union soldiers riding through the streets, vainly seeking forgiveness for their wicked treatment of the town. Still another story recounts a spirit who assailed a local businessman by violently shaking his bed in an apparent effort to stop his home renovation project.

Some of these stories even have a bit of macabre humor mixed in for good measure. There is the poem about the ghost of Founders Hall, who ever laments his lost bottle of whiskey inside one of the structure's stately columns. The ghost narrates, "My splendid jug of old Scotch rye / For many long sad years / Inside 'at fast-sealed column high / Has caused this ghost sad tears." Another tale recounts the phantoms of an old man and woman who constantly bicker with one another in death, as in life.

In all, I think these are interesting stories, and they represent the good, the bad, and the unusual about this charming Alabama town that I love to call my home. I hope you'll enjoy them, too.

Limestone County's original Confederate Monument watches over soldiers' graves in Athens Cemetery.
Photo by Alissa-Rose Clark.

I.
The Deadly Inferno of
1893

In the quiet night of March 20, 1893, Athens townsfolk were suddenly awakened from their slumber by the cries of "Fire!" Climbing from their beds, most not bothering to fully dress, they sped from their doors and raced to save the town as best they could.

The east side of the Athens town square was ablaze. The fire had started in a mercantile store in the middle of the block, and it was rapidly spreading in both directions. At that time, most of the buildings on the town square were made of wood and were packed densely together. Firewalls between buildings were uncommon. As a result, if a fire was not doused quickly, it soon engulfed the dry timber and overcame all efforts to extinguish it.

Drawing water from the nearby well on the courthouse lawn, citizens quickly formed a bucket brigade and began to combat the blaze. However, it soon became obvious that the buildings could not be saved. People rushed into the stores along the street to rescue whatever goods could be saved from the inferno. The bright light from the fire cast eerie shadows on the courthouse lawn just to the west as people hurried to and from the storefronts. The heat from the blaze seared their exposed arms and legs as they worked feverishly.

The editor of the *The Limestone Democrat*, R.H. Walker, later wrote, "We are powerless to describe the awful grandeur and majesty of the devouring element as it wrapped in its embrace one after another of the buildings on the east side of the square. Unable are we to faithfully depict the gallant work of the men, women, and children in the noble unselfishness to serve."

As the consuming fire spread from store to store, the townsfolk noticed cries for help. Two young men were trapped in one of the buildings. According to one account, the men had been sleeping upstairs in one of the stores. The proprietor had allowed them to do so, as was customary, in order to guard against theft and fire. Now, the men were trapped and could not escape. They cried for help, but the townsfolk on the street were unable to help them.

The March 25, 1893, edition of *The Limestone Democrat* recounts the tragedy. *Courtesy of Limestone County Archives.*

As the flames and smoke grew close around them, the men screamed for someone to shoot them and put them out of their misery. The helpless townsfolk on the street drew straws to determine who would perform the act, but none of them could carry it out. The young men were tragically consumed by the inferno. For the rest of their lives, the pitiful cries of those men haunted the bystanders who watched the horrific scene.

"Terrible is the calamity which befell our town," the headlines read. "The east side of the square [is] a mass of ruins." Indeed, as morning dawned, passersby could only gape at the hollowed-out, smoking husks of buildings, looming over the goods and merchandise strewn through the streets. The loss was estimated at $50,000, an incredible sum in the 1890s.

The 1893 blaze would be the most disastrous fire that Athens has ever seen, before or since. Yet it was only one of a series of fires on the town square that burned in the latter years of the nineteenth century. The terrible and repeated conflagrations finally spurred local and state leaders to take preventative action. In 1897, the state legislature allowed the City of Athens to issue bonds in order to construct a system of waterworks, and in 1898, the town formed its first volunteer fire company. A local group of young men assembled the "Knockers Club," whose purpose, like that of the two doomed men, was to conduct nighttime vigils for fire. Athens started a municipal fire brigade in 1907.

Thanks to the able efforts of the Athens Fire Department and Athens Water Services, today's Athens town square is protected from fire as never before. Major fires on the town square are rare in the modern era. But the fires of the 1890s serve as a continual warning, and a reminder of the ever-present danger.

The devastation on the east side of the Athens town
square in the wake of the 1893 inferno.

Photo courtesy of "Antique Athens & Limestone County, Alabama" by Robert Dunnavant, Jr.

In the 1980s, almost a hundred years after the great fire, Limestone County teenagers regularly gathered on the Athens town square, not to fight fires and protect property, but to have fun and socialize. On most Friday and Saturday evenings during that decade, the center of Athens was filled with high school students circling the courthouse in cars and trucks, walking the sidewalks, and laughing on the courthouse lawn. The crowd would dissipate only after midnight.

According to local legend, one Saturday after midnight, only two high school seniors remained to "close down the square." The boys were sitting on the tailgate of a truck parked on the east side of the courthouse grounds. As they said their goodbyes, one noticed something curious in a second floor window across the street.

At first, the young man thought he saw just a reflection of light, but as he watched, the light grew and flickered until there was no mistake that it was a fire. By the time he directed his friend's attention to the flames, they had grown to wreathe the room behind the window, and smoke wafted from the roof. The alarmed boys decided to make a run for the fire department, just two blocks north.

What they saw next stopped them in their tracks.

Two men, not much older than them, writhed amidst the flames, frantically waving and banging on the windowpane. Their mouths indicated they were shouting, but no sound traveled to the teenagers. As the boys watched in horror, the fire consumed the two men. The teens raced to the fire station and alerted the firemen on duty. In moments, the wail of a fire engine pierced the night.

But when the firemen arrived with the boys, there was no flame or smoke. The windows were black and deserted. No figures appeared in them. At the urging of the teens, the skeptical firemen entered the building and made their way to the upper floor. There was no sign of any disturbance. The only thing amiss was the slight scent of smoke in the air, but that soon vanished. When the boys continued to insist upon what they had seen, some of the firemen scolded the two, dismissing them as pranksters.

But the other firemen held their tongues and weren't so sure. For, you see, it is not altogether uncommon for there to be false reports of fire on the east side of the Athens town square. Occasional passersby at night claim to see the flicker of fire in those second-floor windows. A few others swear that the flames are accompanied by the silhouettes of two figures, trapped upstairs and unable to escape. According to local legend, the flames are spectral echoes of past infernos, and the images are none other than the ghosts of the two doomed men who met their fiery demise on that fateful night of March 20, 1893.

The east side of the town square as it appears today.
Photo by Alissa Rose-Clark.

II.

The Ghost of Governor George Houston

The local newspaper called it the "grandest night ever witnessed in Athens." On election night in 1874, townsfolk gathered on the front lawn of Athens resident George S. Houston's stately home just west of the town square. The crowd swelled and loudly called for his appearance. Houston, a 63-year-old, balding man with stern eyes, emerged from the front door. To the sounds of their cheers, he declared "I am at your service, gentlemen."

Strong men in the group stepped forward and, setting Houston atop their shoulders, triumphantly paraded him to the town square. He was accompanied by a host of joyful townsfolk carrying lanterns and torches. The town was ablaze with lights, and the echo of celebratory gunfire rolled through the town.

Mr. Houston had just been elected governor of the state of Alabama. He did so by winning a large majority over his Republican opponent in a record-breaking turnout of voters. His election was of tremendous significance, both then and today, because it marked a break from the oppressive rule of the Radical Reconstructionists, whose heavy taxes and corruption had cast the state into financial ruin after the Civil War.

As the group arrived at the newly built courthouse, Houston was met by the cheers of the town's ladies who had gathered there. The portly Houston, dubbed "the bald eagle of the mountains" by the newspapers, stood amongst them in the lantern light. He promised an end to Republican rule by a sane and conservative administration. Cheers and thunderous applause met his words.

The people escorted Houston back to his home, but the merrymaking continued long into the evening. "We expected the boys to retire because of the lateness of the hour," wrote the editor of *The Limestone Democrat*, "but all night long the loaded anvils and the ring of fire arms sounded."

The front balcony of the George S. Houston Library and House. *Photo by Alissa Rose-Clark.*

Houston made good on his promise to restore fiscal responsibility to the State of Alabama. During his tenure as governor, he mercilessly cut state expenses and slashed the state's debt. He refused to spend vast sums in a contingency fund set aside by the legislature for government purposes. He transformed the state penitentiary from a financial drain into a source of state revenue. Perhaps most significantly, he helped broker a beneficial settlement of the state's tremendous railroad bond debt.

Houston was no stranger to public life. He had previously served as a United States senator. In fact, on the eve of the Civil War, he reluctantly led Alabama's congressional delegates as they presented papers of secession to the federal government. Prior to being a senator, Houston had served in the United States House of Representatives, where he earned the nickname "Watchdog of the Treasury."

In his private life, Houston was a well-respected lawyer in Athens. His law partner and friend, Luke Pryor, another notable citizen of early Athens, wrote that Houston "ascended in unbroken triumph through all grades of life from the humblest walks to the exalted station of Senator" with "honesty, fidelity, unswerving principles, and high sense of honor." Houston was an intelligent, persistent, and eloquent man. Legend has it that he valued punctuality, and tinkered in frustration with a large grandfather clock in the Houston home because it did not show the precise time.

Governor Houston was overwhelmingly elected to a second term. At the end of that second term, he was nominated by the Alabama Legislature to return to the United States Senate, in the same position that he had held before the Civil War. Houston made his triumphant return to Washington, but his second foray as senator was unexpectedly cut short during the first year of his term. It is speculated that Houston fell ill with a cold during a return to Athens. As the illness worsened into emphysema, Houston could not resume his station in Washington and became bedridden on the lower floor of his home. Finally, on the morning of December 31, 1879, lying in bed, Houston woke from sleep and called out, "John, bring me my shoes. I must return to Washington." Those were his last words. He died there in his home.

Governor Houston's two-story framed home looks much the same today as it did when he lived there in the 1800s. The well house, adjoining cabin, and rose garden are lost to history, but the home still stands resolutely facing West Street, now renamed Houston Street in honor of the governor. One can still see the carvings of initials in the eastern windows on the second floor, believed to be cut by one of Houston's daughters with her diamond engagement ring. After some years of disrepair, the structure was donated by Houston's descendants to the City. It is now a public library, known as the George S. Houston Library and House, and it is listed on the National Register of Historic Places.

The home, bordered by tall magnolias within the reach of its balconies, commands respect, as did its former owner. Inside, its high ceilings and glass-blown windows evoke a foregone era. It has many of the features of a home forgotten by time: the smell of old books, and the sight of warped floorboards. It also has the worn sounds of an old southern mansion. The floors squeak and pop as one walks across them. The doors groan as they are pushed open. But there is another sound in this old house that merits special attention.

Governor Houston's grandfather clock still chimes in this old place. It can be heard echoing throughout the house, and it still fails to keep the correct time. The chime for two o'clock may ring twenty minutes too late, and the chime for seven may sound fifteen minutes too soon, but the clock still keeps time in an approximate fashion. The strangest thing, though, about this grandfather clock is that no one can find it.

Rooms and closets have been searched. Walls in the house have been opened. And yet no matter how hard the librarians try, there is no trace of the grandfather clock – except, that is, for its peculiar chime. The chime is most commonly heard when atmospheric conditions are changing, as if it were a barometer of sorts. It may ring, for example, as a harbinger of a sudden temperature change, or immediately prior to the arrival of a thunderstorm. The chime may disappear for months, or it may ring several times in a week.

Portrait of Governor Houston in the downstairs library. *Photo by Alissa Rose-Clark.*

Carvings in a second floor window, believed to be cut by
Governor Houston's daughter. *Photo by Alissa Rose-Clark.*

School children often visit the Houston house on field trips. After
one such excursion, a young boy who enjoyed his visit returned on
Saturday with his mother. The boy rambled through the museum
exhibits on the second floor before returning to the check-out desk at
the front entrance. The child overcame his shyness in order to ask the
librarian a question.

"Yes, dear, what can I do for you?" asked the librarian.

"Well," he explained, "I brought my mother here and I wanted to
show her that big grandfather clock on the second floor."

"I'm sorry," the librarian replied, "we don't have a grandfather clock
in this house."

"Oh, yes you do," insisted the child, "I played beside it earlier this
week."

The chime of the grandfather clock isn't the only unusual thing that
occurs in this house. In addition to the smell of old books, librarians
sometimes catch the scent of hot candle wax, although no candles are

burning, or smell vegetables cooking, although the source of the aroma cannot be found. Moreover, librarians are sometimes greeted, even in hot summer, with inexplicable pockets of cool air in the upstairs rooms. Some have come to attribute all of these strange occurrences to Governor Houston's ghost.

A room on the lower floor once served as the men's parlor. In Governor Houston's time, after guests had enjoyed an evening meal, the gentlemen would retire to the parlor to enjoy cigars and brandy. Today, rows of books and a few chairs fill the former parlor, and a bulletin board displays community announcements. One morning, a librarian noticed that a slip of paper, earlier tacked to the bulletin board, had fallen onto the floor. Jokingly attributing it to Governor Houston, the librarian scolded him aloud, and asked that he wait until the evening to enjoy the room with his guests. When the librarian closed the doors that night, all of the chairs were in order and various announcements were securely pinned to the bulletin board. When she returned the following morning, however, the chairs had been rearranged, and every single announcement had been removed from the bulletin and scattered across the parlor.

Perhaps Governor Houston's ghost is not particularly fond of changes to the old house. Several years ago, two men were hired to install central air and heating in the old building. This naturally involved lots of work in the attic and subfloor, as the two installed vents and air shafts. Laboring in the hot air of the attic with their flashlights, the two workers heard something rustling behind them. When they turned, however, no one was there. Returning to their work, they heard something behind them once more, this time coupled with the feeling that they were being watched. Seeing no one there, they returned to their work. When it happened a third time, the men thought they caught a glimpse of a figure behind them, in the access panel to the attic. Attributing it to nervous librarians, the men walked downstairs during their next break to reassure the staff about the work being performed. The librarians insisted that they had not been in the attic, and advised the workers to announce to Governor Houston that their appearance in the attic was for the purpose of the improvement of his house.

Several minutes after the men returned (reluctantly) to the attic, they again heard a noise and sensed a watchful presence behind them. They could see someone barely within their peripheral vision, keenly studying their every move. Both men covered their eyes with their hands, as one of the workers said loudly, "Governor Houston, sir, we are only here to try and make your house a better place. Please let us do our jobs!" According to the men, the presence vanished immediately, and they were permitted to continue without any further difficulties.

If the ghost of Governor Houston were involved, it is speculated that the former "Watchdog of the Treasury" may have simply been frustrated by the considerable expense of installing central air and heating in his home. After all, Houston had done quite well without it in the 1800s. Whatever the source of these strange events and occurrences, there is no doubt that the George S. Houston Library and House remains one of the most beloved and significant structures in Athens. In recent years, however, its historical significance is often rivaled by the interest in the supernatural events within its walls.

Second floor room where one can sometimes hear the grandfather clock. *Photo by Alissa Rose-Clark.*

Lithograph of Governor Houston in upstairs bedroom. *Photo by Alissa Rose-Clark.*

III.

The Screaming Ghost of the Vasser-Lovvorn Home

A sudden, shrill scream erupted, and Garth Lovvorn, Sr., jerked awake. He bolted from his bed, groping in the dark for a light. Garth saw his wife lying there – she was fine – but it was clearly the anguished cry of a woman that he had heard. The sound had come from somewhere inside his house. Garth ran frantically into the hall, tripping over furniture. He raced through the rooms, looking around. The screaming began again, and its source was from somewhere above him.

Garth realized that the cries must be coming from his attic. Grabbing a flashlight from a nearby cabinet, he opened the small attic doorway and climbed the narrow flight of stairs. As he entered the dusty attic, he waved his flashlight from side to side. He shouted, "Where are you?" but there was only silence in reply. Garth saw nothing but dusty boxes and trunks.

Suddenly, the loudest shriek of all burst from above him. Fumbling with the flashlight, Garth pointed it directly at the source of the sound. The screaming stopped, as if something had abruptly cut it off. The hair on Garth's neck stood up straight as he saw that nothing was there at all – just an old wooden beam. The scream was terrifying, to be sure, but Garth was remembering something about that wooden beam that was far more unsettling.

Garth was a child when his family moved into the house in 1952. By that time, the house, now known as the Vasser-Lovvorn Home, was already over a hundred years old. The house was built around 1824, only a few short years after the town was founded. As one of its early owners advertised, "[i]t is two stories high, with a basement story containing a dining room and cellar, well-ventilated and grated. The lot has about one acre and a half of ground and has a great variety and abundance of fruit." The home passed through the hands of several owners, until it was purchased in 1846 by Richard W. Vasser.

Mr. Vasser was a man of great wealth and reputation in the early years of Athens. He came to the town with his parents in 1819 and began working as a store clerk. Vasser saved his money until he had enough to start what would eventually become known as the "R.W. Vasser and Co." mercantile firm. From that point, he enjoyed tremendous financial success, making shrewd investments at every turn. In fact, Vasser became known as the "merchant prince of Athens." As one contemporary said of him, "[Vasser] was a man of the highest sense of honor, and thought it a disgrace to any man not to pay an honest debt. … He possessed more influence perhaps than any man in Limestone County, and could elect any man to office he might desire." Vasser had several children, including his daughter, Pattie. According to tradition, Pattie Vasser was a beautiful and passionate woman.

The Vasser family, like many other families, experienced the cruel hand of fate during the Civil War. In 1863, the family abandoned their house in war-ravaged Athens to be nearer to the Vasser sons, who were soldiers stationed in Georgia. However, Pattie's oldest brother, Harry, died in Jonesboro from wounds received in several battles. Another brother, Joseph Price, experienced terrible war injuries that would eventually claim his life as well. In 1864, Pattie's father took ill and

The Vasser-Lovvorn Home. *Photo by Alissa Rose-Clark.*

died in Atlanta before he could return home. Upon the war's conclusion, the remaining family, including the 23-year-old Pattie, returned to Athens and tried to adjust to the war's aftermath.

For a time, it appeared that Pattie's fortunes had improved. After the Civil War, she fell desperately in love with Lieutenant Robert McClure of the Confederate Army. The two were married on a cold Valentine's Day night in 1866. They spent several happy months together. But on November 2, 1866, only about nine months later, Pattie's hopes for a better life took a turn for the worse.

According to legend, on that autumn morning, Pattie was at the Vasser home without her husband. A few days earlier, Robert had announced that he was traveling to see his family in Clarksville, Tennessee. Pattie had felt uneasy about his planned trip, and begged him not to go. After enduring so many tragedies in her young life, Pattie was no doubt very protective of her loved ones. But Robert had left anyway, laughing and assuring Pattie that he would soon return safely. Then, on the cold morning of November 2, there was a knock at the door, and a courier delivered a telegram. It contained devastating news, reporting that Robert had died the night before. Pattie dropped the paper to the floor and burst into tears. Pattie's family gathered about her and offered tender words, but she was inconsolable. Bolting from their arms, she raced upstairs and barricaded herself inside the attic. With her family pounding on the door and struggling to gain entry, the young woman found a rope. Standing atop a chest, she threw the rope over a long wooden beam that stretched across the attic's width, and feverishly fashioned a noose. Then, placing it around her neck, Pattie leapt into the air. As she did so, she let loose a terrible, anguished scream. The cry was heard throughout the house, filling her family with dread. Pattie's shriek, though, was abruptly cut short as the noose jerked tight around her neck. Her family burst into the room and witnessed the terrible sight.

Although Pattie unleashed her pitiful cry in 1866, many claim that it can still be heard from the attic of the Vasser-Lovvorn Home. It comes during the late and still hours of the night, and there is typically no warning. It is not heard regularly, and sometimes several years may pass between occurrences. But, as Garth discovered that dark night in the attic, while the scream may be predisposed to lengthy interludes, it has lost none of its potency over the decades. It remains just as jarring and clear as it must have been on the fateful day that Pattie received her telegram.

The Lovvorn family has reported other bizarre happenings over the years. During one period, it was almost routine for the family to return home from an outing and find that the parlor doors, closed when they left the house, had been opened while they were gone. Indeed, on a few occasions, the family was present when the doors opened, and they experienced the distinct feeling that someone entered the room with them – although nothing at all could be seen. One night, a family friend bolted through the house in a panic after seeing the ghostly image of a person watching him from a doorway. On another evening, an occupant woke from a deep sleep to find that someone was tickling his feet, but when he looked down to spy the culprit, he saw nothing there.

Another inexplicable event happened on November 29, 1976, when Garth's son, a small child at the time, heard his father's footsteps racing up the stairs. This was unusual, since it was the middle of the day when his father was normally at work. Thinking that his father had returned home for lunch, the boy called out to him. When Mrs. Lovvorn, who had also heard the sound of footsteps on the stairs, heard no reply, she walked through the house looking for her husband. She found that all of the doors were locked, and that she and her son were the only people in the house. Picking up the telephone, she called the bank where Garth worked. He answered the phone and explained that he hadn't been home that day.

Although these strange events had been evenly interspersed throughout the years, at one point in the late 1970s, they virtually stopped. Indeed, they grew so infrequent that some townsfolk claimed the haunting had run its course. As a local historian wrote during that period, "[t]he doors have behaved quite well within recent years" and "[t]here have been no sounds from the attic in a long time."

A window from the attic where some have heard the
haunting shriek. *Photo by Alissa Rose-Clark.*

Not long after those words were written, the phenomena returned in full fury. The incidents – the doors, the screams, and the strange noises – suddenly began to happen on an almost-daily basis. Whatever spirits inhabited the home were clearly agitated and restless.

During this time, the Lovvorn family realized that there seemed to be a connection between the mysterious happenings and the ongoing construction at the house next door. That neighbor's house, located immediately to the east, was the only thing standing between the Vasser-Lovvorn home and the old Athens Cemetery, the final resting place for some of the city's earliest inhabitants. Most of the markers in the graveyard are now below ground, and the ones that remain above the surface are in many cases illegible and shattered. There are a few exceptions, including one small, well-preserved corner of the cemetery that belonged to a single family – the Vassers. Several impressive monuments remain in this private area, including four cracked granite tombs. Richard Vasser's body was returned from Georgia and buried here, as were the bodies of his sons, Harry and Joseph. One can also see Pattie's name on one of the tombstones.

For as long as anyone could remember, there had been a dirt path connecting the Athens Cemetery to the backyard of the Vasser-Lovvorn home. Undoubtedly, the trail had been created by the Vassers themselves, who made regular visits to the family gravesites. However, the path remained long after the Vasser family left the home. It was considered an unusual trail because although it appeared to be trod regularly, that was not the case. Local storytellers maintain that the way was free from grass and weeds because the spirit of Pattie Vasser walked each day from her grave to her home.

Whatever its nature, the path could not resist the construction of a rear addition to the neighbor's house. The addition blocked the trail entirely, obstructing any direct travel between the cemetery and the Vasser-Lovvorn Home. When the neighbor's construction was completed and the path was interrupted, the screams, opening doors, and strange noises stopped again, just as suddenly as they had started.

Vasser family tombstones on the grounds of the old
Athens Cemetery. *Photo by Alissa Rose-Clark.*

Almost twenty years elapsed without further incident. Once again, it seemed that whatever ghosts haunted the old house were finally at peace. There was speculation that the neighbor's rear addition had done what the old noose could not – that Pattie Vasser's cries had been silenced forever.

Then, in 2002, Garth began his own remodeling project. He hired workers to construct a rear addition to his house, almost twenty years after his neighbor's similar project. The endeavor would involve demolishing part of the old rear walls, and making significant alterations to the structure of the Vasser-Lovvorn Home. Upon the project's completion, the last remnants of the old path would be gone.

One night in the midst of the construction, Garth was jarred awake from sleep by the sudden and violent shaking of his bed. It jerked with such force that Garth almost fell out of it. Then, the movement stopped. No source for it could be found. Garth thought it was only his imagination, and so he returned to sleep.

The following day, the builders continued their work. That evening, once again, Garth awoke to find that his bed was rocking, but less emphatically than the night before. Garth grabbed the sides of the bed to hold on tight, and the shaking stopped.

The next day, the workers resumed their efforts, including the demolition of the old rear walls. That night, Garth's bed shook again, almost pitifully, and with less force than before. As it gently swayed back and forth, Garth jumped to his feet, and turned on his lamp. Looking at the foot of the bed, he cried, "That's enough!" As if in response, the shaking stopped.

Since that night, Garth has never been shaken awake again. In fact, there have been no more inexplicable footsteps, no more phantom tickling, and no more ear-piercing screams erupting from the attic. Indeed, many people now believe that the apparition is gone, that the haunting, after so many years, is finally over.

But they have believed that before.

The grave of Pattie Vasser. *Photo by Alissa Rose-Clark.*

IV.

The Many Ghosts of Founders Hall

Founders Hall at Athens State University is widely considered to be the most impressive edifice in the city of Athens. The towering, white Greek Revival structure is the oldest of all the school buildings. For many years, it was the only building on campus. It was built by the collaborative efforts of the city's townsfolk in 1842-44. Founders Hall now houses administrative offices, parlors, and a chapel. It is often requested as a site for weddings and other celebrations.

Founders Hall has an important place in the rich history of Athens. It is a reminder of the importance of education to the people of the community, who rallied to found a female academy almost immediately after the beginning of the town in 1818. The very land on which it sits was donated for this purpose by John McKinley, who would later serve as a justice of the United States Supreme Court. During the Civil War, academy students watched the Battle of Athens from the building's second floor.

Remarkably, this grand structure somehow escaped the destruction wrought in 1862 by Union Colonel John Turchin's invaders. Legend has it that Yankee soldiers intended to burn Founders Hall, and were approaching it with torches in hand when Madame Jane Hamilton Childs, the legendary school headmistress, met them on the front lawn. From the folds of her long black dress, she produced a handwritten letter from President Abraham Lincoln. The note instructed the

Union soldiers that no harm should come to Founders Hall or to its students. Colonel Turchin cursed the letter, but spared Founders Hall nonetheless.

Founders Hall has been rumored to be haunted for well over one hundred years. Some of the earliest tales of its apparitions date back to only a few years after its construction. It is said, for example, that in the mid-1800s, a professor was seeking a job at the school. After a very satisfactory day of touring the grounds and interviewing with the president, the professor lay down to sleep in a bedroom on the second floor. A few hours later, the professor was awakened by the sounds of clanking chains and footsteps outside his chamber door. The man was so frightened that he left Founders Hall before dawn. The professor refused to return to the school, even after he was offered the job.

Students of Athens Female Academy standing beside Founders Hall in 1905. *Photo courtesy of Athens State University.*

A similar incident occurred almost a century later as a young professor worked late into the night. Writing at his desk, he heard footsteps and a sound like the rattling of keys. The sounds came from outside his office door. Thinking that perhaps a security guard was coming to check on him, the professor opened the door, only to be greeted by something completely unexpected. Looking into the hallway, he saw a smoky, gray vapor only a few feet before him. It seemed to take form and then slowly melted into the darkness.

Many people claim to have seen mysterious balls of light appearing in the air above Founders Hall. It has become almost commonplace for school officials to be shown photographs, taken at a wedding or a festival, that depict strange glowing objects. Those enthralled by the paranormal claim that these luminous orbs are the manifestations of spirits, who gather to experience the joy and excitement surrounding such social events.

A. Mary's Lantern

A well-known legend of Founders Hall involves a young woman named Mary and her ill-fated romance. During the Civil War, Mary was a student at the school, then known as Athens Collegiate Institute. She lived in the dormitory on the third floor of Founders Hall.

A beautiful girl, Mary attracted the attention of a handsome Confederate officer. The two entered into a whirlwind romance and could hardly bear to be apart. However, the couple's plans were often thwarted by Madame Jane Hamilton Childs, the school's stern headmistress and the same bold woman who had confronted the advancing Yankees at Founders Hall. Madame Childs was known for her strict enforcement of the school's curfew and rules concerning fraternization with the opposite sex.

One cold autumn night, circumstances forced Mary to risk her headmistress' wrath. Earlier that day, Mary learned that her lover's regiment had been ordered to leave Athens the following morning. In a desperate effort to see him that evening, Mary sent word that they should meet under the trees in front of Founders Hall at the stroke of midnight. Mary planned to sneak out of the building long after her curfew, expecting that Madame Childs would be fast asleep at that late hour.

The legendary Madame Jane Hamilton Childs. *Courtesy of Athens State University and Alabama Heritage magazine.*

It was almost midnight when Mary opened her door and peered down the hall. Seeing no light from Madame Childs' chamber, she carefully exited her room. As quietly as possible, Mary walked to the stairway at the end of the hall. There, confident that she had not been discovered, she stopped to light her lantern so she could see to walk down the staircase. She lit a match and turned to look behind her one last time. As she did so, the flame caught her dress. Alarmed, Mary frantically slapped at her legs to put out the fire. In her panic, she stumbled over the burning dress and tripped. As she tumbled down the staircase, her lamp fell with her. Its glass shattered, and the splattering oil exploded into flame. Mary's screams woke Madame Childs and the other students as she tumbled downward and crashed at the foot of the staircase. She suffered terrible burns and broken bones, and died soon thereafter.

Occasionally since that terrible night, people have looked into the third floor windows of Founders Hall and seen a yellow light. It travels from window to window, rising and falling as if it were lifted and lowered by human hand. The light cannot be seen from inside the building, and is visible only from the grounds below. It is said to be the glow of Mary's lantern, shining as she travels from room to room searching, even today, for the Confederate officer who was waiting under the trees that night. The lantern's light never leaves the third floor, for even in death, Mary is too afraid to descend the staircase that claimed her life.

Looking down the Founders Hall stairwell from the third floor. *Photo by Alissa Rose-Clark.*

The third floor of Founders Hall, where Mary's lantern is said to travel from window to window. *Photo by Alissa Rose-Clark.*

B. The Night Stalker

There are other strange occurrences at Founders Hall, leaving some to speculate that more than one ghost haunts this old building. Some of the most common unexplained phenomena involve footsteps in empty halls; doors opening and shutting of their own accord; the smell of smoke; and sudden popping, crashing, and clanging sounds. Faculty and students have also reported seeing puffs of black smoke appearing in hallways and then quickly dissipating. Most of the time, these things occur at night and are concentrated on the third floor. The manifestations have been the cause of varying degrees of fear among students and faculty. Even some of the security guards have been known to avoid the third floor at night. Some students attribute these unusual occurrences to a phantom they call "the Night Stalker."

In the 1980s, the inexplicable sounds were so well-known and prevalent that a group of college students set out to record them. They maintained a recording station on the third floor of Founders Hall over a four week period. The audio recorder was set to capture sounds each night, at a time when Founders Hall was empty. At the end of the period, the students eagerly compiled their findings. Many faculty and students were not surprised by what they heard on the recordings – strange groans, footsteps, pounding noises, and creaking sounds.

During this same period, another group of students claimed to have made contact with the ghostly entity responsible for the sounds. After hearing a story about a female student's encounter with a boy that appeared and then disappeared in her dormitory closet on the third floor, the group set out to discover what they could about the mysterious Night Stalker. The students gathered on the third floor of Founders Hall around a table and attempted to communicate with the ghost through a séance-like exercise. The students claim that the entity made itself known to them by seizing the table, lifting it from the floor, and tapping on it in a series of answers to their questions. From this encounter, the students reported that the ghost was the spirit of a young boy. (Indeed, a beloved stable boy is fondly remembered in the oral history of the school, and some speculate that this spirit is that same boy.) The boy had worked in the school's horse stables in the early years of the college. In life, the youth had loved Founders Hall. He had spent considerable time examining its nooks and crannies, and would often hide in the shadows to watch the grand parties held in its parlors. His childhood had abruptly ended, however, when he was kicked in the head by a horse and died. As a spirit, the youth could not bear to be parted from the school that he loved. So his spirit remained at Founders Hall, and continued to explore and watch.

The students reported that it was the boy's curious and mischievous nature that spurred his ghost to make itself known to students and faculty. His manifestations, they explained, mirrored the boy's experiences in life. The black smoke and related smell were said to invoke the blacksmith's shop. Likewise, the sounds of banging metal were of horses being shod. The popping noises were the sounds of stable whips.

The third floor hallway of Founders Hall, home of the legendary "Night Stalker." *Photo by Alissa Rose-Clark.*

C. The College Ghost's Jug of Whiskey

One of the most persistent legends involving Founders Hall relates to a lost jug of whiskey. According to legend, the jug belonged to a talented brick mason who directed the construction of the four massive columns at the front of the building. The brick mason, a slave whose name is lost to history, was well known for his craftsmanship. He was supposedly fond of his "likker" and brought a jug of scotch whiskey to work with him one morning in 1842. As he began constructing the brick base of one of the columns, he stashed his jug in the hollow center. Then, he turned his attention to the next column and started its base as well. When he came back to the first column, he found that the bricks had grown so high that his jug could not be retrieved. According to legend, that jug of whiskey still lies within the hollow interior of the northernmost column at Founders Hall.

Over the years, other men have made claim to the jug. One of the most prominent was James M. Brundidge, who supervised all of the exterior construction of the building. (Strangely enough, Brundidge's claim was reported in his obituary.) Another claimant was James L. Raney, a carpenter who claimed to have placed the jug inside the columns to keep it cool.

The location of the hidden jug is also the subject of some dispute. The columns are named for the Four Gospels, Matthew, Mark, Luke, and John, in order from the north to the south. The most common location for the jug is said to be in Matthew, but other sources claim it is in Luke. Whatever the source or location, the legend of the lost jug of whiskey remains prevalent in the lore of Founders Hall.

The lost jug of whiskey is more than just a curious artifact. It also has been suggested that the jug serves as nothing less than the motivation for the ghost of Founders Hall. This ghost, it is said, is the brick mason, obsessed with protecting the jug from those who would plunder it for their own enjoyment. With one foot in mirth and the other in the macabre, an anonymous student author wrote the following poem about this ghost in the 1911 school yearbook:

The Spirits of Athens

The watchman is a man of might,
  The cook, he is a host,
But I'm the one who rules by night,
  For I'm the College Ghost.

O, I was once a mason proud
  With a wicked taste for drink,
For that I come to wear a shroud
  And make the livin' shrink.

I worked upon the columns high
  Before the college door
I brot my jug, 'twas mighty dry
  And hid it in the core

Of that tall column on the left
  And when no boss was by
I'd grab the jug with motion swift
  And swing it up on high –

And take a nip with eager zest
  To wet my dusty throat.
'Twas old Scotch rye, the very best
  A mason proud could boast.

The boss he was a temp'rance man
  And played a cruel trick:
He broke into my pleasant plan,
  To haul a load of brick.

I went away and hauled the brick
  And then I brought some sand,
But O, it was a cruel trick
  The cruel boss has planned!

Another mason had been set
    To build the column high,
Tho in its core was goods to wet
    A throat like mine, dust dry.

And not until the column high
    Was finish'd, capped, and crowned
Did that mean boss permit me by,
    Or let me hang around.

Student illustration from 1911 school yearbook.
Courtesy of Athens State University.

For 20 years I watched the spot
    Where my good jug was hid,
A-hopin' that a fire hot
    Might ope that fast-sealed lid.

When the years had passed, I died
    From grief for that good gin,
And inna ground I would not hide,
    But prowl, a bogey thin.

The four columns of Founders Hall – Matthew, Mark,
Luke, and John. *Photo by Alissa Rose-Clark.*

My splendid jug of old Scotch rye,
    For many long sad years
Inside 'at fast-sealed column high
    Has caused this ghost sad tears.

And still I guard the sacred spot,
    Because in this same town,
There's others hope a fire hot
    May free my jug renowned.

They's some as scramble out-o-bed
    When they hear the fireman cry,
A-thinking now that I am dead
    They'll get my good Scotch rye.

But still their hopes I'll surely fool;
    I'm watchful at my post.
I'll save my jug, an' save the school,
    For I'm the College Ghost.

In gleamin' ghostly garments white
    I wander o'er the house,
A-stealin' through the dead o'night
    A-wanderin' about.

I never scare the girls in bed
    With ghastly, ghostly shout,
Nor make them think they see the dead
    A-wanderin' about.

But I watches o'er them kindly,
    And quiets their alarm,
And I never lets them blindly
    Rush into dreadful harm.

And I likes my job o'bein'
    Just a simple College Ghost,
And of watchin' close and seein'
    All's right, upon my post.

Student illustration from
the 1911 yearbook.
*Courtesy of Athens
State University.*

Whether the unexplained phenomena at Founders Hall are caused by the forlorn ghost of Mary, the lonely stable boy, the brick mason who lost his liquor, a combination of all three, or none of the above, are questions left to the reader. Indeed, no one has ever suggested that only one ghost can haunt a building at a time. Whatever one's conclusion, however, there can be little doubt that Founders Hall remains the source of many unexplained and strange manifestations.

V.

The Phantoms of McCandless Hall

A. Abigail Burns' Last Great Performance

The best known ghost story in the city of Athens involves venerable McCandless Hall at Athens State University. McCandless Hall has been the home of fine arts at the college since its construction in 1912-14. It is a stately Greek Revival structure whose chief feature is its large auditorium with proscenium arch and upper balcony.

In the early twentieth century, McCandless Hall was, as it is today, the frequent site of student concerts and theatrical presentations. It also served as a host to traveling musicians, actors, and other performers. Musical performances were especially frequent – newspapers from that period record visiting opera companies, orchestras, instrumental soloists, and others. These shows were very popular among the citizens of Athens, and the McCandless Hall auditorium was often filled with spectators from both the college and the community.

Perhaps the most memorable evening in the grand history of McCandless Hall involved the performance of Abigail Lydia Burns. Abigail was a beautiful, golden-haired singer who came to Athens along with a theatrical troupe in 1914, not long after McCandless Hall was constructed. She was an aspiring opera singer, on tour as preparation for that goal. Her troupe's reputation for a good show was well known, and by the third and final night of the performance, McCandless Hall was packed beyond its capacity. The audience members greatly enjoyed the operatic performance, but their hearts were especially captured by the beautiful Abigail. At the conclusion of the evening, she took the stage for a solo singing performance. As Abigail concluded her song, the enamored audience erupted into a thunderous, standing ovation. Their cheers and applause shook the building.

So great was their adoration and so vocal were their cheers that Abigail was forced to return to the stage for repeated curtain calls. Well-wishers threw red roses onto the stage as a sign of their love for the young actress. The audience's applause did not subside until Abigail, so moved by this outpouring of affection, raised her hand to speak. The crowd hushed to listen. Then, standing in a white dress and holding a bouquet of red roses, an emotional Abigail vowed "to return to McCandless Hall again, even if it is the last thing I ever do."

Soon afterwards, Abigail left McCandless Hall, along with the rest of her group, to travel to their next engagement. It was a stormy evening, and not far from Athens, the group encountered a terrible thunderstorm. Rain and wind battered the horses and carriages, making progress difficult. Then, as Abigail's carriage crossed a bridge over a ravine, tragedy struck. A bolt of lightning crashed nearby and the already-frightened horses bolted in panic. As they did so, the carriage disengaged from the horses and burst through the bridge's wooden rails. The carriage plummeted into the chasm and burst asunder on the rocky floor below. Abigail was crushed beneath it.

Her comrades raced to the wreckage. Pelted by rain, they frantically removed the debris until at last they discovered Abigail. Her white dress was tattered and torn, yet she still clung tightly to the bouquet of red roses. Her fellow actors pulled her broken body from the shattered vehicle. They marveled at her last words. As Abigail lay in their arms, she whispered to them: "I have a promise to keep."

McCandless Hall. *Photo by Trisha Black.*

When the news of Abigail's death reached Athens, there was an outpouring of grief. At the college, a beech tree was planted in her memory. It still stands today, as one college professor noted, "in mute testimony of the town's endless affection for an actress they loved and embraced as their own."

Not long after Abigail's death, strange things began to happen at McCandless Hall. Students, especially those pursuing the theatrical arts, began seeing odd visions in the windows, shadowy shapes that appeared and then moved away. They also heard footsteps in the building when no one else was there. Occasionally, students on stage would be in the middle of a performance and be overcome by the sudden fragrance of roses, when no flowers were present.

The most striking claim, however, comes from students who have looked into the second floor windows above the main entrance and reported seeing the image of a beautiful woman with golden hair. The woman, bathed in warm light, wears a white dress and holds a bouquet of red roses. Upon second glance, she is not there at all.

Legend has it that the vision is none other than the ghost of Abigail Burns, making good on her vow to return to McCandless Hall – perhaps for a final performance of sorts. And to this day, she still carries the bouquet of roses given to her by admirers, and the memory of her last great production.

B. Love's Fatal Leap

There are some who claim that Abigail Burns' promise to return to Athens was inspired by something other than the reception she received from the townsfolk. Those who have studied the legend closely maintain that Abigail was in love with a wealthy young man she had met during her stay in the town, and that she had promised *him* that she would return. If this is indeed the case, then Abigail's story is not altogether unlike the story of the other apparition who haunts McCandless Hall.

In the early twentieth century, McCandless Hall, like the other campus buildings, was normally not accessible by men. The school was

Tree planted in memory of Abigail Burns. *Photo by Trisha Black.*

a female academy, and males were admitted only upon appointment or invitation. As its administrators no doubt intended, this made it very difficult for boys to see the female students that they admired. However, enterprising young men regularly schemed to skirt the campus restrictions.

Such was the case with one young man in the early years of McCandless Hall. He longed to see the pretty girl he considered to be his one, true love. Aware that she practiced playing the organ at a particular time of night, he snuck into McCandless Hall that afternoon, hid in the balcony overlooking the stage, and waited. When she sat down to play, the young man planned to leap to the stage and dramatically take her into his arms.

The young man remained hidden for hours. Finally, the girl arrived. His anticipation mounted as he peered down and saw his love take her seat at the organ. He knew that she thought herself alone in the building. As she began to play, her admirer rose to his feet and climbed the railing. However, just as he was preparing to leap, she glanced up and saw him towering above her, a menacing shadow crouched to jump. She screamed in fright, and in doing so, caused the young man to lose his balance and fall. He crashed onto the floor below, his arms outstretched for the pretty maiden who sat just beyond his reach. The fall took his life.

Two recent incidents have been connected to this tragic event from the past. McCandless Hall has a lower floor located directly underneath the auditorium and its stage. On one recent occasion, a student was working late at night in this basement area when she was startled by a loud booming noise that shook the ceiling above her. Alarmed, she rushed upstairs to investigate the source of the crash, but found nothing out of place. Although the crashing noise was heard by many inside the building, no cause for the sound could ever be determined. The location of the crashing noise, however, was determined to be just underneath the edge of the balcony and beside the McCandless Hall stage.

View from the stage inside McCandless Hall. *Photo by Alissa Rose-Clark.*

Months later, another incident occurred at McCandless Hall. A community band was on stage during a practice session. Suddenly, one student musician's face became white and she stopped playing her instrument. Recovering later, the terrified student explained that in the middle of the practice performance, a young man dressed in a long coat and top hat appeared floating above the tops of the audience seats. She reported that he glided across the auditorium, then into and through the wall at the north end of the theater.

Some say these are spectral manifestations of the man who fell from the theater balcony. The booming noise is presumed to be the sound of his body crashing into the floor. And it is believed to be his phantom that the young musician saw floating over the theater seats. If this is so, then they would be added to a long list of the ghost's appearances.

Indeed, the young man is said to have never left McCandless Hall. He has been seen throughout the decades since the 1920s. Most often, he has made his presence known as a shadowy shape hiding in the corner of the balcony, spied by those rehearsing from the stage below. Sometimes, he also has been seen by audience members sitting in the balcony, who turn aside for a moment and find a young man staring at them from the shadows. Believers claim that in death, the young man lingers on at McCandless Hall, forevermore wrapped in frustration and unrequited love for the girl organ player who remains just beyond his reach.

View from the balcony inside McCandless Hall. *Photo by Alissa Rose-Clark.*

VI.

The Heroine of Brown Hall

In the final months of 1909, a typhoid epidemic struck the city of Athens. During the very early twentieth century, typhoid fever was still a frightening disease in America. Vaccination for the illness was not widespread, and cases were often fatal. The sometimes poor hygiene and sanitation practices of that era, combined with the concentration of people in cities, contributed to the spread of the awful disease.

When untreated by modern medicine, victims of typhoid suffer terribly. Initially, the disease is characterized by a rising temperature, combined with listlessness, coughing, and headaches. A victim may also experience a bloody nose. Then, as the typhoid progresses, red spots may appear on one's torso. A person becomes incapacitated with high fever and severe abdominal pain. In the final stages of typhoid fever, terrible complications can occur, including intestinal hemorrhage and encephalitis.

In October, 1909, this malady struck hard at Athens Female Academy. When school officials discovered the outbreak, they immediately ordered that all students return to their homes wherever possible. The faculty also left the school. However, several students were already too sick to travel. Many of them were just children, admitted to the preparatory school, between the ages of twelve and fourteen.

One brave teacher could not bear to leave the sick children. Her name was Florence Brown. She was a 20-year-old woman from Vinemont, Alabama. Florence served the academy as a literature teacher and college bookkeeper. Her parents were natives of Canada, and she was their only child.

Florence labored hard to comfort the sick children. She also permitted herself to be quarantined with them in an effort to protect others from the spread of the disease. Four of Florence's young charges died while in her care. However, after those tragic losses, the others' symptoms slowly began to ease and they gradually recuperated. There is no doubt that an exhausted Florence experienced great relief as those survivors were finally sent home.

It appeared that the epidemic was finished, and that life at the academy would soon return to normal. However, the typhoid soon returned with a vengeance, as Florence discovered that she had contracted the disease. The brave young woman succumbed to it, and died. Reporting later to the school trustees, academy President Mary Norman Moore wrote that "[o]ne of the saddest [deaths] of the number was that of ... Miss Florence Brown, a young American girl of English and Canadian parentage . . . less than twenty-one years of age."

Ultimately, 65 persons took ill, and 15 students died in the typhoid epidemic. (Eleven students perished after being sent home from the academy.) School officials suspected that the outbreak had originated in the kitchens, from a careless worker who prepared food for the students. Further investigation also implicated the city's water supply, furnished by an uncovered spring in the heart of town. Soon after the epidemic, the spring was covered, and other measures taken to prevent possible contamination.

Florence's legacy was preserved by President Moore, who led efforts to construct a new Greek-style campus building to be named "Florence Brown Hall," in memory of Florence's service to the children. Florence's parents made significant financial contributions to the cost of the building. It was constructed to be a dormitory, and contained a reception hall, fireplaces, three bathrooms, and twenty-six rooms. Brown Hall was ready for students by the fall of 1912.

Brown Hall. *Photo by Alissa Rose-Clark.*

Brown Hall has served many purposes over the years. Since its initial period as a dormitory, it has been used as the college president's home, for classrooms, and now, as the central administrative offices for the university. It has been remodeled several times, but it still appears much as it did in 1912.

Florence Brown's legacy at Athens State University does not end with Brown Hall. Indeed, her ghost is said to roam the campus, with its primary presence in the building that bears her name. To students, she is thought of as a watchful guardian. When sororities met in Brown Hall, their members often saw Florence at the door while they gathered. Others described her standing protectively outside their dormitory rooms as they slept. In this way, her apparition has been described as "gentle" and "benevolent."

To the faculty, however, Florence's ghost has conveyed a different attitude entirely. She is viewed as a gremlin of sorts. Missing keys, locked doors, rearranged items, and computer glitches are often blamed on her. When the administrative staff moved into Brown Hall, an art teacher who had taught in the building for several years warned a newcomer, "Don't ever stay too late because strange things happen here." When pressed to explain himself, the teacher advised that he often taught a late class in the evening. He recounted that he would often put objects down, certain where he had placed them, but then be unable to find them later. He explained that when he finally located the items, they would be far from where he had left them.

The professor dismissed these incidences to chance until one particular night when he became convinced that something supernatural was occurring. He had just finished a late-night art class, and all of the students had left the building. As the professor packed his things to go, he noticed a rattling sound coming from a nearby wall. Approaching the noise, he realized it was coming from a picture frame. The frame was vibrating on its own, with no apparent cause. As he studied it, he saw that other things in the room had begun to rattle. Indeed, he realized that some kind of invisible wave had formed, intensified, and was traveling around the room. As it passed the objects in its path, they violently shook. Some even jumped right off the wall and crashed onto the floor. The phenomenon continued, moving steadily around the room until it completed an entire circle, stopping where it had started. In its wake, trashcans were overturned, frames were tilted or shattered, and books were strewn across the floor.

The contrast between the protective apparition guarding students and the irksome poltergeist bedeviling professors has led some to speculate that these occurrences actually involve two entirely different spirits. Others are convinced, however, that this is not the case, and that all of these matters can be attributed to Florence Brown's ghost. The differences are easily explained, they contend, when one appreciates the last few days of Florence's life. Her devotion to the students was apparent to all who knew her. Less apparent, say the storytellers, is that Florence was privately aggravated with her fellow faculty members for abandoning their posts while she remained with her charges. Although she ultimately faced death itself for her bravery, her peers returned to the academy with little inconvenience. Therefore, legend holds that although Florence's ghost walks primarily as a guardian of the students, she cannot resist the occasional harassment of faculty members when she recalls their predecessors of over a century ago.

VII.

The Ghost Who Loved Mice Figurines

Have you ever put an item down, and then when you returned to retrieve it, it was gone? Most people have had such an experience. But not many people have felt it quite like Ruby Lovelace.

Mrs. Lovelace lives in a house on the corner of Madison Street and Market Street in Athens, just a block from the courthouse square. Her house, constructed in the early 1900s, is a sturdy home with tall ceilings and broad supports. It has endured much over the years, surviving the ordeal of a fire in the 1920s and the abuse of tenants in the 1990s.

Mrs. Lovelace is enamored with her home. She moved into it in the early 1990s, but circumstances forced her to move away soon thereafter. She could not forget it, however, and so she eagerly returned to the house as soon as circumstances allowed. Mrs. Lovelace loves the structure's period fixtures, its side porch, and its thick wooden floors. She is also fascinated by its other curiosities, not the least of which is its ghost.

She certainly didn't believe there was a ghost in the house when she moved into it. Indeed, she saw nothing out of the ordinary as she unpacked her things. But it didn't take very long for Mrs. Lovelace to realize that there was something quite unusual about the place. Her suspicions started when she began to misplace common household objects, only to find them in unusual places. Although this involved different kinds of items, more often than not it involved her jewelry.

Mrs. Lovelace is accustomed to placing her jewelry at her bedside table before she lies down to sleep. Almost as a ritual, she sits down on the bed, removes her earrings, necklace, and rings, and places them on the nightstand. Then, she turns out the lamp and goes to sleep. When she wakes in the morning, Mrs. Lovelace sits up in bed, and puts the jewelry back on.

One night, not long after she moved in, Mrs. Lovelace engaged in her bedside routine. The next morning, she reached for her jewelry. She put on her necklace and rings, as usual, but then she noticed that her earrings were missing. When she couldn't find them beside her bed, Mrs. Lovelace assumed she had absentmindedly misplaced them. She was not concerned when she discovered her earrings later that day on the kitchen table.

Mrs. Lovelace's beloved home. *Photo by Alissa Rose-Clark.*

She did think it was curious, however, when the same thing happened the following day. Once again, she had placed her jewelry on the nightstand in the evening, and once again, a piece of her jewelry was missing the following morning. This time, however, it was her necklace that was gone. As before, she discovered the missing necklace later that day somewhere in the house.

This phenomenon became something of a pattern. Hardly a day went by without a piece of her jewelry disappearing and then reappearing somewhere in the house. At first, Mrs. Lovelace began to think she was becoming increasingly forgetful, and she became a bit worried about her own health. As the incidences continued, however, she began to suspect that something strange was happening in the old house. Yet it was never a chief concern of hers – that is, until the experience involved her mice figurines.

Mrs. Lovelace loves mice figurines. She has quite a collection. Her mice come in various colors, shapes, and sizes. Some are plastic, some are glass, and others are porcelain. There are tiny collectibles, not much bigger than a thimble, and large models, about the size of a grapefruit. Some are antiques, some are new, and a few carry special sentimental value. She keeps them in her kitchen, many of them inside a wooden curio cabinet with locking doors.

One afternoon while she was cleaning her house, Mrs. Lovelace removed three of her mice figurines from the display cabinet to dust them off. She left them on the kitchen table when she was finished. She remembered them as she lay in bed that evening, and resolved to place them back inside the case the following morning. The next day when she awoke, she opened her eyes to see them sitting right beside her on the bed stand. Mrs. Lovelace couldn't endure any more of this phenomenon. Frustrated by whatever was going on in the house, she angrily shouted, to no one in particular, "OK – you can mess with my jewelry all you want – but you leave my mice alone!" No sooner had the words left her mouth than she felt a bit silly. After all, no one was there. She put the mice back in the curio cabinet and locked its door.

As she went about her business that day, she forgot about the incident completely.

The next morning, she woke up, put on her jewelry, and walked into the hall leading to the kitchen. Just as she entered the hallway, something crunched beneath her feet. She stopped, looked down and discovered that it was one of her mice collectibles. And it wasn't alone. Mrs. Lovelace was startled to see three or four more figurines strewn throughout the hallway leading to the kitchen.

As she carefully walked through the kitchen doorway, she saw that the rest of her mice – indeed, her entire collection of figurines – were scattered to and fro across the room. Some were on the floor, and others were on the kitchen table. Only a very few figures remained inside the curio cabinet. The cabinet's door remained locked, just as it had been when she left it the night before. "Fine," Mrs. Lovelace stammered aloud. "You can touch whatever you like."

Since then, Mrs. Lovelace has not complained one bit when objects turn up in places they are not supposed to be. She doesn't doubt her state of mind any longer. Instead, she recognizes the strange occurrences as an interesting curiosity of her beloved house. She thinks it possible that something or someone is sharing the house with her, although she is quick to point out that she had rather not confront it face to face.

Her family, as one might expect, thinks the house is haunted. Some of them claim that the home is frequented by the ghost of a Mrs. C.W., who resided in the house decades ago. This theory took shape one morning in the mid-1990s when a friend of Mrs. Lovelace was visiting. While walking down the hall to join Mrs. Lovelace in the kitchen, the friend became aware of someone behind her. Turning, the friend saw an elderly woman standing in the foyer. The woman was wearing a grey dress and had a strange, almost confused look in her eyes. Thinking that she had come through the front door to see Mrs. Lovelace, the friend welcomed the woman and led her down the hall to the kitchen. The friend then turned to call for Mrs. Lovelace, but when she looked back again to the silent visitor, the old woman was gone. She had vanished, and a search of the house turned up nothing.

This strange visitor met the description of Mrs. C.W., a former occupant of the house in the early 1900s. Mrs. C.W. was described by those who remembered her as a kind but sad woman, who had faced many tragedies in life. She had also loved the old house a great deal. It was another remembrance of Mrs. C.W.'s life, however, that garnered the most attention by Mrs. Lovelace's family. Mrs. C.W., it is said, had lost many of her possessions in the house fire that was mentioned earlier, not the least of which was her jewelry and figurine collection.

A part of Mrs. Lovelace's mice figurine collection.
Photo by Alissa Rose-Clark.

VIII.

The Haunted Cabins of the Beaty-Mason House

$\mathcal{A}t$ the corner of Beaty Street and Green Street stands one of Athens' oldest and most beautiful homes, the Beaty-Mason House. It was built in 1826 by Robert Beaty, one of the chief founders of the town. It was occupied by Beaty's family and descendants until 1958, when it was donated to Athens State University. Today, it serves as the home of the school's president. At the rear of the Beaty-Mason House, along the edge of its well-manicured backyard, stands a much smaller structure. It is a saddleback house made of logs, with a chimney in the center that provides heat for the two rooms on each side. At one time, the house was actually two separate cabins with a common wall, and housed servants to the family in the main residence. These cabins have been considered haunted for over a century.

In the late 1800s, after the Civil War, an elderly man and woman worked for the residents of the Beaty-Mason House and lived in these cabins. One was a cook named Betsy, and the other was a handyman named Mark. Betsy was a warm and outspoken woman who was very spiritual and superstitious. On the other hand, Mark was worldly and practical. He was a friendly but embittered man whose wife, the love of his life, had betrayed and left him. He never considered marriage again. Betsy and Mark were friends, but they constantly bickered. Their loud arguments could often be heard erupting from the cabins.

Historian Elva McLin reports that Mark would say something to the effect of, "Look at that moon up there with a ring around it. Gonna rain tomorrow."

Betsy would reply, "Don't you start nothin' about that moon. God, he's got a man up there listenin' to you. That ring says you got one day to mend your ways."

Mark would snap back, saying, "Ain't no room up there for a man. That moon's about as big as a nickel; wouldn't even hold baby Jesus."

Then Betsy would storm away, muttering, "Can't tell that man nothing. Devil's gonna get him for sure."

Mark would also turn away, fuming, saying, "Fool woman. Don't know nothing and don't want to."

Log cabins behind the Beaty-Mason House.
Photo by Alissa Rose-Clark.

Betsy claimed that she heard ghosts at night as she lay in the cabin, and Mark scoffed at her. In 1954, Miss Mary Mason, a noted town historian and preservationist who lived in the Beaty-Mason House, wrote of her childhood in the years around 1900, recalling:

> Betsy … waited on my grandmother in those days so long ago. The cabin is double. Betsy lived in one and Mark, our cook in the other, and although it was built in 1826 no doubt to this day the timbers pop and settle far into the night. Well, Mark was somewhat disdainful of Betsy's lower intelligence, and was ready to fight when someone asked him if Betsy was his wife (both were very small of stature). But as I was saying, the house would pop at night and Mark told me he heard Betsy say "Git off de roof sperrits, and go back to de graveyard whar you belongs. All time walkin on me'-all's roof." If she believed in ghosts here was proof that she was not afraid of them.

Betsy and Mark died long ago, but their spirits are still said to haunt the old cabins. Visitors to the property have often experienced cold spots inside the old log structure. Sometimes one can hear the inexplicable sounds of crashes and pops coming from inside. Others have heard still stranger noises. At a party hosted by the college president in the 1980s, a guest stepped outside the Beaty-Mason House for a breath of fresh air. While walking in the backyard, he heard the soft sound of singing coming from inside the old cabins. Thinking his host had prepared entertainment for the party, he approached to listen. He heard what he described as an old spiritual hymn, softly sung by male and female voices in a beautiful melody. A door to the structure was unlocked and so he opened it and looked inside. When he did, however, the singing suddenly stopped and he saw only a vacant and dark chamber.

The man's experience is not unique. On quiet nights, neighbors can still sometimes hear the sound of singing coming from inside that old structure, although it has been unoccupied for many years. Other times, though, the noises emanating from the cabin are not melodious at all. Passersby have infrequently reported hearing the sounds of male and female voices shouting and arguing. Believers claim these are the voices of Betsy and Mark, who, to this day, continue to sing and debate with one another as the decades pass them by.

The whereabouts of Betsy and Mark's graves are unknown. There was once a burial plot for servants on the vast, original grounds of the Beaty-Mason House. However, as the estate was sold in piecemeal fashion, the Mason family caused the graves to be opened and the bodies to be moved elsewhere. Some of those bodies may have been moved to a burial chamber underneath the Beaty-Mason House. A former resident of the house once told of such a room, and explained that it had been sealed away from the rest of the house by a brick wall.

That brick wall stands in a dark corner of the basement beneath the Beaty-Mason House. In years past, it had a dark spot that could not be lightened, although the area was repainted again and again. Some said that, if you listened closely at the wall during the night, you could hear the rattling of bones coming from behind the bricks. Legend has it that during one dark and stormy night, one or more elderly spirits removed those bones from behind the wall, and reinterred them in a flower garden outside, closer to the cabins. There was no trace that the wall had been disturbed, but the dark spot completely disappeared. Although some have attributed this act to another, others speculate that this was the handiwork of Betsy's and Mark's ghosts, who, when it came to the question of their final resting place, were finally of one accord.

Inside the log cabins. *Photo by Alissa Rose-Clark.*

Looking upward from the log cabins. *Photo by Alissa Rose-Clark.*

IX.

The Family Spirits of the Donnell House

To the casual visitor, the Donnell House seems out of place. The beautiful old two-story "T" style house, with its four square stately columns, is surrounded by the worn campus buildings of Athens Middle School. Yet, given its long and important place in the history of education in Athens, this is a very appropriate location to find the Donnell House. The structure served as a school for boys in the late 1800s, a public high school from 1936-1950, and thereafter, as the residence of the city's superintendent of education until 1970. Local preservationists saved it from deterioration in the late 1970s, and caused it to be placed on the National Register of Historic Places. Today, it is regularly used by the community for special events such as weddings, showers, receptions, and banquets. The Donnell House is often manned by a curator, and is available to the public for tours.

Several years ago, a couple visiting from out of town wanted to explore the historic structure. They entered the front door, which was unlocked, and stepped inside the foyer. They planned to begin their visit with the gentlemen's parlor, and approached the door to that room. As they did so, however, a man exited the parlor and noticed them. Smiling warmly, he introduced himself as the Reverend Robert Donnell. He was later described as an "austere gentlemen" who was wearing "old-fashioned clothing." Donnell advised that he was conducting a Bible study in the parlor. The couple apologized for their interruption. Donnell assured them that no apology was necessary, and politely thanked them for visiting. He invited them to tour the house on their own and return to the room later.

After the couple had roamed throughout the house, they returned to the parlor. The meeting had finished by that time and so they entered the chamber. Brilliant sunlight poured from the windows into the room. Reverend Donnell, who was still inside the parlor, greeted them again and commented that the room "was much too bright for his taste." After a short visit with Donnell, the couple thanked him for his hospitality and left the house.

Years later, the same couple passed through town and visited the Donnell House once again. This time, they were met at the door by the curator. After exchanging pleasantries, the couple shared the story of their previous visit to the home. The wide-eyed curator was astounded by the tale. The Reverend Donnell had certainly lived in the house that still bears his name, but he had died – in the year 1855.

Reverend Donnell built the house in 1845, and lived there with his family. He was active in the ministry of the Cumberland Presbyterian Church, and he was known as a hard-working and impressive speaker. Even after his retirement, Donnell continued to preach, sometimes delivering up to four sermons a day in gospel meetings. After his death, one of his friends lamented the loss of this effective orator, explaining that "[i]f Robert Donnell could come back to earth and preach ... just one such sermon as I have heard him preach at the camp-meetings it would set the whole vast thing on fire ... ." While there are no tales of Donnell's spirit returning to the Donnell House to deliver sermons, returning to lead a study in the parlor appears to be another thing altogether.

The Donnell House. *Photo by Alissa Rose-Clark.*

But the reports of ethereal gatherings in the gentleman's parlor pale in number to the reports of unusual events from the second floor of the home. The rooms of the Donnell family's children were located in that level of the house. When Reverend Donnell died, he bequeathed this house to his only son, James Webb Smith Donnell. James and his wife raised fifteen children in the Donnell House.

Nannie Donnell was one of those children. She and her sisters occupied the North Bedroom on the second floor. In May, 1862, young Nannie took ill and was confined to a bed in that room. Her mother spent many days and nights tending to the sick teenager.

The bedroom's window looked out over a vast lawn that stretched from the house westward to the old Huntsville Stage Road. It was from this window, beside her ailing child, that Nannie's mother watched Union soldiers invade Athens during the Civil War. The woman must have been aghast as she saw the Yankee troops turn off that stage road and onto the spacious grounds surrounding her home. The soldiers struck camp all across the wide lawn, and from this base of operations, brutally ransacked the town. The marauding soldiers were commanded by Colonel John Basil Turchin, who infamously invited the destruction by telling his men, "I see nothing for two hours."

Portrait of Reverend Robert Donnell. *Photo by Alissa Rose-Clark.*

Later, celebrating their success, federal troops underneath Nannie's window loudly played music and sang throughout the night. The shadows from their campfires danced across the ceiling of her bedroom. Their braying tunes and drunken shouts terrified the poor girl. Nannie's mother, fearing for the health of her daughter, called from the window and told the soldiers that there was a sick girl in the room. She explained that Nannie was near death and pled with them to be quiet. In response, the soldiers erupted into laughter, and one shouted back at her, "Better she should go to Heaven listening to Yankee music!" Local legend has it that the replying soldier was none other than Colonel Turchin himself, who had set up his headquarters on the Donnell lawn and happened to be walking nearby.

After several encounters such as this, Nannie's mother, outraged by the soldiers and exhausted from tending to her daughter, went to Nannie's bed and pulled a full chamber pot from underneath it. Passing back to the window, she registered her defiance by pouring its entire contents onto the soldiers below. Although the carousing soldiers quickly vacated the area underneath the window, it was too late for Nannie. She died shortly thereafter. On May 18, 1862, a local diarist made this entry in her journal: "Nannie Donnell died Friday. She was sick when the Federals came, & the fight & constant noise & excitement, I suppose, killed her …"

Today, Nannie's second floor room has been recreated as a nursery suite, complete with antique toys, to illustrate its role in the Donnell House's history. It is a pleasant space, but it is often the source of strange incidents. Visitors to Nannie's bedroom often claim that they have encountered spots in the room that are inexplicably cold. Some describe a foul odor that sometimes enters the room, the source of which cannot be found. Others claim that just entering the room fills them with anxiety and sadness. From the downstairs parlors, when everything else in the house is quiet and still, some of the regular volunteers often hear the sound of doors opening and closing, as well as the unmistakable squeak of footsteps on the bedroom's wooden floor. These happenings, among others, have caused persons familiar with the house and its history to claim that the ghost of little Nannie Donnell haunts the second floor.

On some occasions, persons in the downstairs rooms have clearly heard the sounds of playful laughter coming from that bedroom, and, less frequently, the sound of a child crying. After such noises, the bedroom is almost always inspected by its caretakers. Although no person is ever found to be the source of the sounds, curators will sometimes find that certain objects in the bedroom are out of place or strewn across the floor. Those objects are often toys.

Antique toys in Nannie Donnell's bedroom.
Photo by Alissa Rose-Clark.

Nannie Donnell's bedroom window. *Photo by Alissa Rose-Clark.*

X.

The Strange Gentleman and the Abandoned Well

Don Ussery walked down the interior hallway. The building was quiet. It was early in the morning, and, as usual, Don was the first one to arrive at work. He stopped to open a locked door which led into one of the work areas, and then stooped down to secure a doorstop. As he did, he glanced inside the doorway to the break room tables, shelves, and nearby stairway. From the corner of his eye, Don saw that he wasn't alone. Someone was standing just feet away from him, a few steps up the stairway. The person was leaning on the rail, and watching him closely. Don was a bit startled – he hadn't expected to see anyone in the building this early. He stood to speak, but the man was gone.

Don thought that he must have been imagining things, and silently laughed at himself. He stepped inside the door and looked down. There, beside the break room table, part of the hardwood floor had been removed and strips of wood and debris cluttered the area. A clear plastic sheet, foggy and scattered with beads of water, was draped across the gaping hole. Construction workers were in the process of replacing the hardwood floor and re-securing a long-abandoned well that was situated underneath the building.

Although the area where Don stood is now a corporate break room at the rear of scores of cubicles, it was once a small outdoor area, at the rear of two important and colorful buildings. One of them, the Jones Building, fronted Market Street. At the turn of the twentieth century, it was one of the town's busiest saloons. Later, it became a shoe shop and the home of various mercantile businesses. Just to the west of the Jones Building, and situated on the corner of Market Street and Marion Street is the Hendricks Building. The Hendricks Building was constructed in approximately 1902, and for many years, housed one of the city's most prominent hardware and grocery stores. The Hendricks Building abuts the Jones Building, but it runs longer and deeper, extending at one point beyond the Jones Building and then turning east in an "L" shape to reach completely behind the Jones Building. There was once a gap between the rear of the Jones Building and the Hendricks Building, and in that gap, a small outdoor area. A well had been dug long ago in this area, and local historians believe that it served both buildings, as well as others in the immediate neighborhood.

On that morning in 2008, when Don looked across the floor of the break room and thought he saw a strange visitor, the well had been abandoned for many long years. Both the Jones Building and the Hendricks Building are now the home of an impressive technology firm. After a terrible fire gutted the Hendricks Building in 1994, local businessmen acquired both buildings and reconfigured their interiors. By that time, the Jones Building had already been extended to cover the old well. When the buildings were completely renovated, the owners placed a hardwood floor over the old water source. However, as the years progressed, the wooden boards on that floor began to buckle and twist due to the moisture emerging from below. Consequently, a construction crew was retained to reseal the abandoned well and repair the floor.

The Hendricks Building. *Photo by Alissa Rose-Clark.*

When he arrived the next morning, Don wondered if the crew had finished their work. Again, he was the first one there, and again, he unlocked and opened the door to the break room area. He had already forgotten about the man on the stairs from the previous day. But there it was again – the image of a man watching him open the door. Don placed the doorstop and slowly entered the chamber. The floor was still gaping open, the plastic sheet still spread across the top of the abandoned well. The room was still and silent. There was clearly no one in the room or on the stairs.

The strange and disconcerting image of the man caused Don to recall other odd things that had happened in the building, all of which, he realized, occurred within a few feet of the old well. He remembered stories about objects that moved on their own, such as an empty chair that had inexplicably rolled across a room to situate itself at a table full of people in the middle of a conference call – as if someone else were joining the meeting. He recalled a co-worker who felt someone brush into her from behind, who turned and looked but saw nothing there.

Don also remembered when, not too many months earlier, he had been working alone late one night in the Jones Building. As he worked in his cubicle that evening, he had heard a sound from the rear of the building, only feet from the site of the well. It sounded very much like someone tinkering with the coffeepot. Don recalled gliding backwards from his desk on a rolling office chair so that he could peer down the long building. Seeing nothing, he returned to work. Moments later, however, he stopped again when he heard the sound of someone approaching from the rear of the building. He couldn't hear footsteps, but he clearly recognized the creak and groan of the old wooden floor as the person took each step. When he heard the creaks stop behind him, he slowly turned to see who it was. No one was there. Don quickly gathered his things and left his work unfinished for the night.

Don Ussery's viewpoint when he saw the strange gentleman on the stairs. *Photo by Alissa Rose-Clark.*

The staircase where the figure stood and stared at
Don Ussery. *Photo by Alissa Rose-Clark* .

Don thought about those experiences and anecdotes all throughout
the night after his second sighting of the man on the staircase. By the
following morning, he was determined to get a better look at this
strange visitor. Again, he came in as usual, disarming the security
system, turning on the lights, and preparing the building for a new day.
Again, he unlocked the door to the break area and slowly pulled the
door open. But this time, as he stooped to pick up the door stop, Don
focused his attention on the periphery of his vision. There, standing
only a few steps up the stairway, an impeccably dressed gentleman
watched Don closely. The man was dressed in a dark suit and vest,
reminiscent of the early 1900s. He had a handlebar mustache, and
wore a black bowler hat. His hands were crossed and resting on the
stair rail. The man had an interested, but calm, look upon his face.

As slowly as he could manage, his heart pounding in his chest, Don turned his head to face the man. As he did so, the apparition slowly faded from view. Yet Don was certain that the man had not moved, not even slightly. He investigated the stairway, but the figure had left no trace of his presence.

Bemused and amazed, Don stepped into the hallway. Needing some fresh air, he walked towards the exit. Doing so, he moved past a long row of antique photographs, spaced evenly down the hall. The photos depicted the Jones and Hendricks Buildings as they appeared over a century ago. Further down the corridor, one of the photographs caught his eye. It was a photograph of the storefront of the Hendricks Building in the early 1900s. Standing behind a pony hooked to a wagon were six men, most of whom appeared to be owners or proprietors.

Don suddenly froze. One of the men looked eerily familiar. There, looking at him from the antique photograph on the wall was the very same face of the man who had vanished just moments earlier.

That afternoon, the work on the abandoned well was completed. It was securely sealed, and the floor boards were nailed down tight. The well-dressed gentlemen did not appear the following morning, and he has not been seen since.

The antique photograph hanging in the Hendricks Building hallway. The gentleman that Don Ussery recognized is the second man from the right. *Photo by Alissa Rose-Clark.*

A closer view of the gentleman in the antique photograph. *Photo by Alissa-Rose Clark.*

XI.

Colonel Turchin's Phantom Riders

Sometimes on foggy evenings in the wake of thunderstorms in Athens, the ghosts of Union soldiers can be seen riding down Clinton and Washington streets. On those humid nights, some have claimed to hear the clip-clop of their horses, and others say that the soldiers have sad, mournful looks on their gaunt faces. "It's Turchin's Thieves," an old-timer might say, "seeking forgiveness for their wicked ways."

The name "Turchin" invokes the chief villain in the history of the city of Athens. His given name was Ivan Vasilovitch Turchinoff, although he had anglicized it as John Basil Turchin. He was a Russian-born immigrant with a strong accent, and he spoke only broken English. Turchin was a burly man, bombastic and opinionated. A former colonel in the Imperial Guards of Russia, Turchin came to the United States in the 1850s after becoming friends with George B. McClellan, who would later become commander of the Union Army during the Civil War. On May 2, 1862, as a colonel in the United States Army, Turchin invaded Athens with a brigade of Union infantry and engaged, in the words of a Cincinnati newspaper, in "outrages unfit to be named."

Turchin and his troops had been part of an occupying force in nearby Huntsville, under the command of Union Brigadier General Ormsby M.

Mitchel's 3rd Division. When a band of Union infantrymen was flushed from Athens by Confederate cavalry, Mitchel directed Turchin to capture the town. Mitchel was angered after hearing rumors that townsfolk had jeered and fired shots at the retreating soldiers. He ordered Turchin's brigade "not to leave a grease spot" where Athens stood.

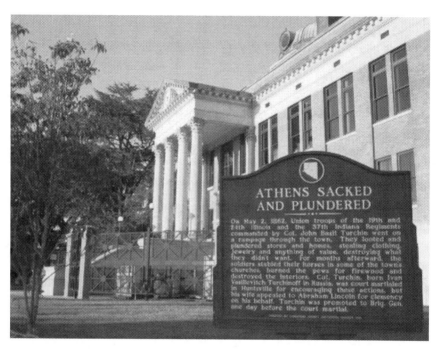

A historic marker on the lawn of the Limestone County Courthouse recounts Turchin's 1862 assault on Athens. *Photo by Trisha Black.*

Armed with that task, Turchin marched his men westward to Athens. The colonel must have viewed Mitchel's comments with satisfaction. Turchin did not mind treating civilians, in his words, "a little roughly." He believed that the southern people were "guerillas" who "pretend to be peaceful, but who are plotting treason all the time." Turchin called the conflict a "war of extermination." With these notions in mind, Turchin's brigade marched in columns towards the city.

The citizens of Athens were ill-prepared for Turchin's threat. For the most part, its townsfolk had only reluctantly accepted secession, and resented that the question had not been put to a vote of the people. Many felt that the division of the Union had been a mistake, and hoped for reconciliation. Indeed, Athens congressman George S. Houston had presented notice of secession to the federal government with tears in his eyes. More than a week after the Alabama Legislature adopted its Ordinance of Secession, the United States flag had been raised atop the courthouse to a one hundred gun salute. W.L. Yancey, the Montgomery leader of the secession movement in Alabama, was even burned in effigy by a large crowd on the public square. Although passions cooled and Athens' citizens had resigned themselves to the inevitability of the Confederacy in 1862, sympathy for the United States remained strong among many.

But things were about to change.

The Union soldiers came from two directions. One group arrived from the east, traveling along Forrest Street, passing beside the old Athens Cemetery and in front of the Vasser home. Another came from the southeast on Clinton Street, stopping to stack arms and set up artillery in the front yard of the Donnell House. At around 9 a.m., leaving a reserve at the Donnell property, Turchin and his men pressed on in the direction of the Athens town square. Nervous townsfolk watched the army from their windows. Some men dared to witness events from alongside the road. Turchin himself warned one young man sitting on a fence, "None of your laughing or jeering," and then promptly had him arrested. Turchin angrily threatened others, saying "I would as soon cut your throats as not."

Arriving at the town square, the soldiers fanned out into the streets surrounding the courthouse. Then they assembled in formation. Turchin rode his horse up to the brigade's adjutant. He reportedly asked, "Ashutant, pas der regiment hungry und fatigued?" The administrative officer replied in the affirmative. Turchin turned in the saddle to face his men. According to some Union soldiers, he raised his voice and shouted, "I shut my eyes for two hours und ton't see nottink!"

John Basil Turchin. *Photo courtesy of the Chicago Historical Society.*

The soldiers erupted from their formations. They burst into nearby stores and looted their stock. Ms. Mary Fielding, an Athens resident, wrote in her diary that "[t]hey broke open Mr. Pete Tanner's store, Mr. Peck's and Mr. Turrentine's stores, Mr. Allen and Mr. Jones' drugstores, Mr. Danforth's shop and ever so many offices and just destroyed, took away and gave away... everything." One group of men plundered an office and scattered a stock of two hundred fine Bibles, trampling them in the street. Others spent their time breaking into safes at the rear of the businesses. Turchin himself seized a pair of silver spurs. As one soldier was leaving a business with his booty, Turchin stopped him to ask, "Hello Company K; you got something nice, hey?"

The men expanded their rampage from the town square to nearby residences. They burst into homes, plundering clothing, food, and valuables, while the terrified citizens watched. The soldiers wantonly destroyed photographs, carpets, windows, or whatever struck their fancy. Others were given to more vicious behavior. While raiding one home, marauding soldiers caused the woman of the house to have a miscarriage which resulted in her subsequent death. At another, they raped a young mother. A soldier remarked, "Colonel Turchin allowed us to take our revenge, which we were not slow in doing, although it was not his orders, still he winked at our proceedings."

Another Union sergeant later wrote that "[a]t the end of two hours there was not much of value to be seen in Athens. Not during the remainder of the war was such wanton destruction of property seen by those men." During the upheaval, Turchin claimed he had been riding about the town. (According to legend, Turchin's destructive intentions had only been thwarted on the steps of Founders Hall, as explained in Chapter 4.) When it was over, amidst the shambles, he ordered his men to clear the streets. Then, no doubt satisfied by what he had seen, Turchin had lunch and took a nap at a local hotel.

Turchin was later court-martialed for his actions. Local witnesses testified against him, despite his complaints that the "testimony of rebels" was not legitimate. Although Turchin was found guilty and dismissed from military service, he was also promoted to brigadier general while the proceedings were ongoing. He received a hero's welcome at his home in Chicago, and then returned to the army a year later, helping General Grant, fittingly enough, rampage through Georgia.

The city of Athens was changed by its experience with Turchin and his brigade. It took many years to recover from "Turchin's Thieves," and any lingering bitterness about secession was replaced with a fervor for the Confederacy. The townsfolk of Athens never forgot Turchin. As Mrs. Fielding wrote in her diary, "I have a perfect contempt for … Turchin, every way." Almost thirty years later, in 1891, a letter to the Athens newspaper reported that "We do not know just how it happened, but a railway train came along and smashed the very life out of the cowardly villain." That rumor turned out to be false. However, when Turchin was confined to an insane asylum in 1901, it was front page news in Athens. The headlines of the local newspaper proclaimed "Gen. Turchin Insane!" The paper recalled Turchin's visit to Athens as a "hideous nightmare" and advised that "[t]here are none to weep . . . over the dire misfortune that has befallen the Russian renegade." Turchin died two months later. Today, a historical marker on the southwestern corner of the courthouse lawn reminds the townsfolk of Turchin and his raiders. Moreover, a local civic group is developing a theatrical production about Turchin's court martial for presentation in McCandless Hall during the sesquicentennial of the Civil War. Indeed, the people of Athens have never forgotten about Turchin.

And Turchin has never forgotten the people of Athens.

Some people claim that on foggy nights in the wake of thunderstorms, one can glimpse the ghosts of Turchin's soldiers traveling into town along Clinton and Washington streets, just as they did those many years ago. Those few brave souls who have been close enough to the apparitions describe them as sad, mournful spirits in tattered uniforms, who stare beseechingly toward the homes on either side of the street. Legend has it that they are repentant spirits who feel regret and anguish over their torment of the town, and that their stares are aimed at the same properties they raided during the war.

GENERAL TURCHIN INSANE.

It Was He Who Planned the Attack on Huntsville.

Chicago, April 11.—A special to the Tribune from Nashville, Ill., says:

"Brigadier-General John B. Turchin, soldier, scholar and author, is insane and confined in the county jail in this city, whence he will be transferred to the Anna Asylum tomorrow.

The above notice will be of interest to the older people of this town and county who were here in the bloody days of the civil war, when this Russian, clothed in the power of a federal officer of high rank, came to Athens with his bloody gang of cut throats and sacked the town and then closed his eyes for two hours, allowing the villians who made up his command to do as they pleased with the good people of Athens. Their visit to

The April 11, 1901 edition of *The Alabama Messenger* announced Turchin's fate to the citizens of Athens. *Courtesy of the Limestone County Archives.*

A few people even claim that chief among the riders is the ghost of a heavy-set Union officer, who looks at the town with haunting, crazed eyes. They say it is none other than the ghost of the infamous Turchin himself, doomed to ride the streets of Athens forevermore, vainly seeking forgiveness for his cruelty during the Civil War.

About the Author

Shane Black lives with his wife, Trisha, and their two children in Athens, Alabama. He was reared on a cotton farm in Limestone County, and has lived in that county for most of his life. He is a 1994 graduate of Birmingham-Southern College, and a 1997 graduate of the University of Alabama School of Law. Shane practices law with the firm of Hand Arendall, L.L.C.

Bibliography

In addition to interviews and oral tradition, the following works were consulted in writing this book, and are recommended to the reader.

I.   The Deadly Inferno of 1893

Dunnavant, Jr., Robert. *Antique Athens and Limestone County, Alabama: A Photographic Journey 1809-1949.* Pea Ridge Press, 1994. p. 81.

Walker, Jr., Robert Henry. *History of Limestone County.* Athens: Limestone County Commission, 1973. p. 158-59.

Westmoreland, Jr., Frank G. *Tales from the Front Porch.* Airleaf Publishing, 2006. p. 81-89.

Bryan, Bob. "Athens square hit by three fires in 1893-97." *Athens News Courier* 4 April 1982.

"Our Town Past and Present." *Limestone Democrat* 15 January 1925.

II.   The Ghost of Governor George Houston

Walker, Jr., Robert Henry. *History of Limestone County.* Athens: Limestone County Commission, 1973. p. 140-43.

George Smith Houston House and Library. *Pamphlet.*

Ostrom, Carol. "Listing Now Official for Houston Library." *Athens News Courier* 13 August 1986.

Owed, Thomas McAdory. *History of Alabama and Dictionary of Alabama Biography*. Chicago: S.J. Clarke Publishing Company, 1921. p. 848-51.

Dunnavant, Jr., Robert. *Historic Limestone County*. Athens: Pea Ridge Press, 1995. p. 109-12.

Webb, Samuel L. & Armbrester, Margaret E., eds. *Alabama Governors*. Tuscaloosa: University of Alabama Press, 2001. p. 101-06.

Limestone County Heritage Book Committee. "George Smith Houston." In *The Heritage of Limestone County, Alabama,* edited by the Limestone County Heritage Book Committee. Clanton: Heritage Publishing Consultants, Inc., 1988. p. 232-33.

Edwards, Chris & Axford, Faye. *The Lure and Lore of Limestone County*. 1st ed. Tuscaloosa: Portals Press, 1978. p. 45-47.

III.   The Screaming Ghost of the Vasser-Lovvorn Home

Axford, Faye Acton, ed. *The Journals of Thomas Hubbard Hobbs*. University: University of Alabama Press, 1976. p. 39.

Edwards, Chris & Axford, Faye. *The Lure and Lore of Limestone County*. 1st ed. Tuscaloosa: Portals Press, 1978. p. 16-17, Addenda 7.

Axford, Faye Acton, ed. *"To Lochaber Na Mair": Southerners View the Civil War*. Athens: Athens Publishing Company, 1986. p. 168, 203 (Diary of Eliza Jane "Piggie" Fielding).

Maddox, Lyndi. "Path threatened, spirits are astir." *Athens News Courier* 31 October 1980.

IV.   The Many Ghosts of Founders Hall

Slate, Joe H. *Psychic Phenomena*. Jefferson: McFarland & Company, Inc., 1988. p. 176-79.

McLin, Elva Bell. "Athens Female Academy/Athens State University." In *The Heritage of Limestone County, Alabama,* edited by the Limestone County Heritage Book Committee. Clanton: Heritage Publishing Consultants, Inc., 1988. p. 22.

Edwards, Chris & Axford, Faye. *The Lure and Lore of Limestone County.* 1st ed. Tuscaloosa: Portals Press, 1978. p. 25-27.

"The Tale of the College Ghost." *The Oracle.* Athens State University, 1911.

Cook, Sandra. "Founders Hall." Alabama Ghostlore. <http://facstaff.uwa.edu/ab/founders.htm>.

McLin, Elva Bell. *The History of Athens State College, 1821-1994.* Nashville: Rand-McNally, 1994. p. 17-29, 55-60, 111-22.

V.   The Phantoms of McCandless Hall

Slate, Joe H. *Psychic Phenomena.* Jefferson: McFarland & Company, Inc., 1988. p. 166-71.

McLin, Elva Bell. *The History of Athens State College, 1821-1994.* Nashville: Rand-McNally, 1994. p. 114-16.

VI.   The Heroine of Brown Hall

McLin, Elva Bell. *The History of Athens State College, 1821-1994.* Nashville: Rand-McNally, 1994. p. 114-15, 237-38, 283.

Limestone County Historical Society. *Athens, Alabama – From the Ashes of 1865.* p. 55 (quoting unidentified 1909 newspaper).

Cook, Sandra. "Brown Hall." Alabama Ghostlore. <http://facstaff.uwa.edu/ab/brownhall.htm>.

Slate, Joe H. *Psychic Phenomena.* Jefferson: McFarland & Company, Inc., 1988. p. 171-74.

VIII. The Haunted Cabins of the Beaty-Mason House

McLin, Elva Bell. *The History of Athens State College, 1821-1994.* Nashville: Rand-McNally, 1994. p. 116-18, 144-51.

Edwards, Chris & Axford, Faye. *The Lure and Lore of Limestone County.* 1ˢᵗ ed. Tuscaloosa: Portals Press, 1978. p. 15-16.

IX. The Family Spirits of the Donnell House

Gray, Jacquelyn Procter. *When Spirits Walk.* Author House, 2006.

Limestone County Heritage Book Committee. "Donnell Family." In *The Heritage of Limestone County, Alabama,* edited by the Limestone County Heritage Book Committee. Clanton: Heritage Publishing Consultants, Inc., 1988. p. 142-43.

Malone, Thomas Stith. "'Scraps' Relating to the Early History of Limestone County." *Athens Post,* 1867, No. XVII.

Edwards, Chris & Axford, Faye. *The Lure and Lore of Limestone County.* 1ˢᵗ ed. Tuscaloosa: Portals Press, 1978. p. 7-8.

Axford, Faye Acton, ed. *"To Lochaber Na Mair": Southerners View the Civil War.* Athens: Athens Publishing Company, 1986. p. 52-53 (Diary of Mary Fielding).

X. The Strange Gentleman and the Abandoned Well

Smith, James Croley. *The Store, Industry, and Façade.* Athens: Limestone County Archives, 1991.

XI. Colonel Turchin's Phantom Riders

Bradley, George C. & Dahlen, Richard L. *From Conciliation to Conquest: The Sack of Athens and the Court-Martial of Colonel John B. Turchin.* Tuscaloosa: Univ. of Ala. Press, 2006. p. 109-25, 221-26, 235.

Walker, Jr., Robert Henry. *History of Limestone County*. Athens: Limestone County Commission, 1973. p. 94-118.

Dunnavant, Jr., Robert. *Historic Limestone County.* Athens: Pea Ridge Press, 1995. p. 61-71.

Axford, Faye Acton, ed. *"To Lochaber Na Mair": Southerners View the Civil War*. Athens: Athens Publishing Company, 1986. p. 41-49, 203 (Diary of Mary Fielding).

Dunnavant, Bob. "Arsonists set town aflame!" *Athens News Courier* 19 December 1976.